Canada Votes

How we elect our government

Written by **Linda Granfield**
Illustrations by **Craig Terlson**

Kids Can Press Ltd.

Toronto

Kids Can Press Ltd. acknowledges with appreciation the
assistance of the Canada Council and the Ontario Arts
Council in the production of this book.

Canadian Cataloguing in Publication Data

Granfield, Linda
    Canada votes : how we elect our government

Rev. ed.
Includes index.
ISBN 1-55074-118-7

1. Elections – Canada – Juvenile literature.
2. Voting – Canada – Juvenile literature.
I. Terlson, Craig. II. Title

JL193.G73 1992   j324.971   C92-093974-0

Kids Can Press Ltd.
585½ Bloor Street West
Toronto, Ontario, Canada
M6G 1K5

Edited by Valerie Wyatt
Book design by Michael Solomon
Typeset by Alphabets
Printed and bound in Canada

90 0 9 8 7 6 5 4 3

Acknowledgments

An information book represents only a smidgen of the materials collected and one quickly learns to ferret out the best sources to make the job as painless and pleasurable as possible. Digging for information happily brings choice tidbits, but it also gives birth to welcome, albeit short-lived, encounters with people enthusiastic about what they do. My thanks go to the following people for sharing their spirit and information with me: first, my editor Val Wyatt and the rest of the Kids Can family for offering me yet another opportunity to write and then yellow-slipping me to a proper finished product; to Michael Solomon for a wonderful design and Craig Terlson for his humorous illustrations.

My gratitude is extended as well to Christine Jackson, Director of Communications, and Jacques Mackay and John Enright, Communications Officers, at Elections Canada for bringing their expertise and updated information to this project; to the staff of the Baldwin Room, Metropolitan Toronto Public Library; the staffs of Elections Ontario, the Canadian National Institute for the Blind, and the National Film Board of Canada; Peter Brennan and Don Cameron of the Hansard Reporting Service; John D. Leach of the Clerk's Department at Etobicoke City Hall, Etobicoke, Ontario; and Peter St. Pierre of the Liquor Control Board of Ontario who made the extra efforts needed to learn about that demon rum and the law.

Finally, hugs to Devon and Brian Smiley, who supported this candidate throughout the election-book campaign. Undoubtedly, they will remember to call in some of my campaign promises!

For Cal
with memories of New York
pizza and Ottawa politics

Table of Contents

The Right to Vote   6

Who Can Vote?   8

Who's the Boss?   12

Get on the List!   16

An Unusual Map   18

Let's Have a Party!   20

Parliament   24

Watch Out for Mrs. Smith!   28

Thank You, Nurses!   32

Now You Have It, Now You Don't   34

Lessons From History   36

See How They Run   38

"Getting to Know You..."   42

Run for the Money   44

"How Do I Look?"   48

Say It Louder, Please!   50

Voting Underwater   52

Election Day at Last!   54

After the Doors Close   58

Glossary   61

Index   63

The Right to Vote — Your Right to Vote

Types of government!!

EVERY COUPLE OF YEARS, SIGNS SEEM TO SPROUT ON the lawns of your neighbourhood. Sure, you think, another election — but have you thought about why we have elections? Maybe they're just a way to create more jobs? Maybe they're a waste of time and money? Maybe you don't have to think about them until you're an adult?

Not so.

In a democracy like Canada's, it is the right and privilege of the people to elect the men and women who will govern them. Your right to vote is protected by the Constitution — no one can deny you the right to vote because of your race, religious beliefs or sex. Not everyone on Earth has this protected right. In some countries people are never asked to choose a new government; they are forced to accept whatever group seizes power. They can't cast their votes and throw a person out of office; they must find other ways, such as violence, to make their needs and wishes known.

It's difficult to live with this kind of violence and insecurity. Between June and September 1988, the people of Haiti were ruled by three different governments, each a revolt against the one before. Elections were held but they weren't very fair. Technically, the people had a say but the outcome was decided beforehand. The leaders decided everything in these situations and they did not have to answer to anyone for their actions.

Canada's system of government is based on the British model of *responsible government*. This means that the decisions and acts of the prime minister and his Cabinet (which the prime minister selects) must be approved by a vote in the House and the Senate. Members of Parliament are answerable (or "responsible") to the people of Canada.

Voters must also be responsible. You may have to wait until you are 18 to vote in a federal election, but you are voting in your home or in the classroom more often than you think. Learning about elections and voting makes each one of us a powerful part of our communities and our country.

Get ready to make your mark!

Winds of change

The multiple-party system with regular elections is the method we use to elect a new government in Canada, but it's not the only way a country can get new leadership.

Some countries, such as Cuba, have a one-party system. This means that all the candidates belong to the same party. Voters can choose between candidates, but there is no choice of parties as there is in Canada.

Many countries, including the Commonwealth of Independent States, once had one-party systems. Then, in the early 1990s, the people in these countries demanded and won multi-party systems.

The people of Communist China were not successful in their quest for a democratically elected government. Despite public demonstrations, as of 1992 China remains a one-party nation where voters have little choice. But political situations can change quickly, and it's plain to see that the voters of the world generate a great deal of power. Their voice is impossible to ignore for long.

Who Can Vote?

ONCE YOU'VE TURNED 18, YOU'LL BE ELIGIBLE TO vote. What happens in the Canadian government is then up to you — and 16 million other voters.

In the past, some Canadians were denied the right to vote because of their ethnic origin, sex or religion. People who didn't own property couldn't vote either. Today, you can vote if you are a Canadian citizen, at least 18 years old and your name appears on the *voters' list* drawn up for each election. Your ethnic background, sex and religion have nothing to do with your right to vote.

You can even vote if you're in jail. A prisoner's right to vote is guaranteed by the Charter of Rights and Freedoms. What about the judge who sentences the prisoner? Until

recently, federally appointed judges couldn't vote. They couldn't be involved in politics in any way. In 1988 the judges went to court and won the right to vote.

Getting on the voters' list is an important first step towards voting. But nothing — including the voters' list — is perfect. Sometimes under-age teens find their names on the voters' list by mistake. In 1988, a dog's name was found on the voters' list in a Toronto election. No, it did not vote.

Hang in there! After your eighteenth birthday you'll have won the right to vote — it's guaranteed by law.

So Who Actually Votes?

People sometimes complain that the government doesn't give them a chance to change what they don't like. But not all the people who have the right to vote use that right. What a waste!

- In national (federal) elections, one-quarter of the voters don't vote. (In a U.S. presidential election almost half the voters — 45 percent — never vote.)
- In most provincial elections, even fewer voters vote. (Quebec is the exception; more voters cast ballots in provincial elections than in federal elections.)
- In municipal (city or town) elections, the voter turnout is the lowest of all.

And size isn't everything at election time:

- Smaller provinces such as Prince Edward Island and Nova Scotia have the highest voter turnout.
- A large province, Alberta, actually has the lowest voter turnout in both federal and provincial elections.

Votes...and alphabet soup

This book concentrates on the federal elections in Canada: but as a newly listed voter, you have lots of other people to vote in (or out) of office, too.

• On the municipal (city or town) level of government, you vote for a mayor, councillors, school trustees and local representatives. In some towns people once voted for fence viewers (the person who settled fence disputes between neighbours) and dog-catchers.

• In provincial elections, you elect members of the Provincial Parliament (MPPs). In Quebec, the members of the Provincial Parliament, called the National Assembly, are called MNAs, and in Newfoundland, members of the House Assembly are known as MHAs. And let's add just one more spoonful of letters to this alphabet soup. The members of some other provincial legislatures are MLAs, or members of the Legislative Assembly.

More Chances to Vote

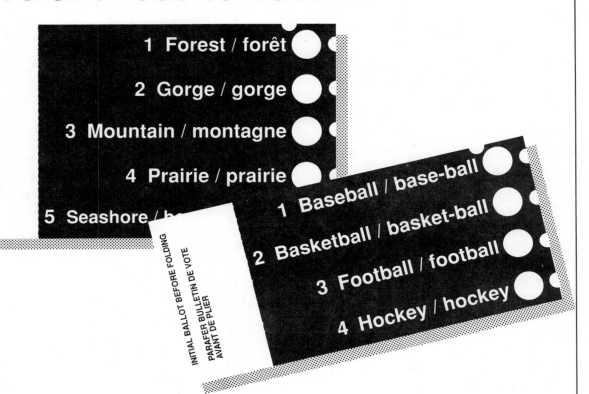

As you've seen, there are plenty of opportunities to get out and vote. By-elections and referendums provide two more chances to have your say.

A *by-election* is a special election held between elections in order to fill vacant seats in a provincial or federal legislature. Sometimes a member dies, retires or becomes ill and is unable to fulfil his or her duties. The voters in the riding still need a spokesperson in Parliament, so a by-election is held to fill the seat.

A *referendum* is a different kind of vote. It takes place when a very important public question must be decided. Most decisions are made by our elected representatives: referendum issues are decided directly by the people. Sometimes the referendum issue is added to the ballot during an election. Other times, a referendum means a separate visit to the polls.

For example, in a city election, the voters in an area where liquor is not sold might vote on the referendum issue of whether to allow the sale of alcoholic beverages. Federal referendums, called plebiscites, are rare. The last one, in 1942, was on conscription (compulsory military service).

Who's the Boss?

Who's Minding the Store?

The returning officers are the key officials in each electoral district. They are appointed by the federal Cabinet. The returning officers co-ordinate the election process in their electoral district. They also set up advance polls, receive candidates' nomination papers and have voters' lists and ballots printed.

SUPPOSE YOU HEARD THAT YOUR FAVOURITE POP star was going to tour in your area. You'd rush to get more information and, better yet, tickets for great seats. Imagine your frustration if you couldn't find out who was in charge of the tour; if everyone you phoned passed you along to another office. The date for the concert was set, yet you couldn't get a ticket. If only someone knew what was going on!

Holding an election is a bit like staging a rock concert. It's a big event that requires lots of organization. Someone has to be in charge. During a federal election, that someone is the chief electoral officer (CEO). It's his or her job to oversee every detail.

The moment an election is called, the CEO contacts all the returning officers around the country so they can start working on the election. Later, formal notification, called writs of election, is sent out. The CEO and his co-workers may have as few as 50 days from the announcement of a federal election to election day. That's

Elections Canada

All federal elections in Canada are organized and run by an agency of Parliament called Elections Canada. This agency is *non-partisan*; that means it is not influenced by and doesn't support any one political party. Elections Canada protects the rights of all Canadian voters to participate freely in each federal election. There are only 50 full-time staff members at Elections Canada to help the CEO. They prepare 600 tonnes of printed material. They send out half a million cheques to pay rentals, salaries and other expenses.

Elections Canada moves with the times. Electronic data processing was used for the first time during the 1988 election. Computers generated up-to-date electoral information quickly and efficiently. Electronic mail saved time and money. One employee sent a letter to 295 returning officers in just three minutes. The same task used to take ten employees a few hours.

REPRESENTATION IN THE FEDERAL PARLIAMENT

CANADA'S ELECTORAL SYSTEM

How It Evolved and How It Works

STUDENT VOTER'S GUIDE

Fourteen million and one, fourteen million and two...

Holding an election in Canada is a big job. Just imagine what it would be like in India, where there are 250 million voters. More than *15 million* ballot boxes are needed for a general election!

not very long to train thousands of poll officers and enumerators, compile voters' lists and take care of millions of voters, voting places and ballots.

Believe it or not, the CEO co-ordinates the entire election — but he can't vote himself! He must remain impartial.

The CEO's job isn't over on election day. After an election, mountains of materials, including all the used ballots, are returned to Elections Canada in Ottawa to be stored. And the CEO must prepare a report for Parliament. Then it's time to get ready for another election!

He or She?

Because Canada hasn't yet had a woman prime minister, the pronoun "he" has been used to refer to the prime minister in this book. In honour of Canada's first woman governor general, Jeanne Sauvé, appointed in 1984, the pronoun "she" is used to refer to the governor general.

Who Calls an Election?

Federal elections must be held at least once every five years. That is the law. But sometimes the prime minister doesn't wait that long. Instead, the prime minister calls an election when he thinks his party is most popular. (Popularity means votes.)

The prime minister must have the governor general's consent to call an election. He asks her to dissolve Parliament and to inform the chief electoral officer of the election day.

The prime minister can choose whatever date he wishes for election day. He will naturally choose a time when his party looks especially good to the public so his party candidates will have a good chance of being elected.

The prime minister will also likely wait until major bills he wants passed have been voted on. He can call the election for any time when he has a good chance of winning. The prime minister's choice of election day is passed on to the governor general who then informs the chief electoral officer.

A federal election may also be called if there is a "vote of non-confidence" in Parliament. This means that the government is defeated in the House of Commons because the members (representing their voters) no longer feel the government is working well. If the government loses the election, it is replaced; if it wins, it continues in office until the next federal election is held.

Get on the List!

SUPPOSE YOU WANT TO TAKE SWIMMING LESSONS. Or maybe you enjoy music and you'd like to attend guitar classes. Chances are you'll have to register beforehand to make sure you can take part in the classes. The same thing happens when you are eligible to vote. First, you have to register by putting your name on the voters' list.

You can register to vote without ever leaving your house. Once an election has been called, specially trained enumerators try to go to every door in Canada and make a list of all voters. The enumerators, who work in pairs in urban areas, represent different political parties. This is so one enumerator won't intentionally leave off the name of a voter who supports the opposing party or add made-up names. Before putting you on the voters' list, the enumerators ask you questions about your citizenship and age. They want to make sure that you are eligible to vote.

Of course, the enumerators might come to your door when you're away. This doesn't mean you can't vote. But now it's up to *you* to get your name on the voters' list.

Announcements are made on television, radio and in the newspapers telling you how to go about getting on the voters' list. There's always a deadline for registering. If you miss it, you won't be able to vote.

Sometimes there are errors on the voters' list. You can still vote after you correct the error. For example, say your name is Joan Smith but, whoops, it appears on the voters' list as John Smith. You don't have to pencil a moustache and fake a deep voice in order to vote. You just have to take the "Oath as to error on List."

After the enumerators have compiled voters' lists, you will be sent a "Notice of Enumeration" card in the mail. This card is very important. It confirms that your name is on the list and tells you where and when voting will take place in your area.

There is one voters' list for each polling station on election day. You can vote only at your neighbourhood polling station where your name is on the voters' list.

An Unusual Map

A North Poll

The most northerly poll in Canada is in the riding of Nunatsiaq, in the Northwest Territories. The Nunatsiaq riding covers more than two million square kilometres, but has a population of only 21,000. Voters receive their election materials by air — ballots and boxes are dropped by parachute!

You could say it's the North Poll. Ho, ho, ho.

YOU'VE SEEN A MAP OF CANADA, RIGHT? BUT HAVE you ever seen an *electoral* map?

This kind of map divides Canada's 10 million square kilometres into 295 electoral districts, sometimes called ridings or constituencies.

If you look at an electoral map, you'll notice that all the electoral districts are not the same size. Why is this?

The country is divided according to the number and location of the people. Each province is allotted a certain number of seats. In 1988 Saskatchewan, for example, had 14 seats, while Ontario, because of its greater population, had 99. Less populated provinces, whether large or small, have fewer seats: Prince Edward Island elects four members and the Northwest Territories and the Yukon

together send three. As the population moves from one province to another or from one area in a province to another, the boundaries have to be changed. For example, in 1987 the electoral boundaries were shifted in all but 13 of 295 electoral districts.

Sometimes an electoral district will grow larger; this means more travel for the candidates who will be campaigning there. The candidates in Nunatsiaq (see page 18) will wear out more shoes covering the riding than the lucky candidates in Quebec's Rosemont riding, where 90,000 people live in only eight square miles.

Polling stations are located within each electoral district so that each poll takes care of about 350 voters. The voters in each electoral district vote for one of the candidates running for election in their area. In the next district, voters vote for different candidates, and so on across the country until all 295 electoral districts have new members to send to Parliament.

Have You Seen My Gerrymander?

In the past, there have been some famous scams concerning electoral district boundaries. One of the most famous happened around 1812 in the United States, when Elbridge Gerry was the governor of Massachusetts.

While Gerry was in office, the boundaries of some electoral districts were redrawn so that his party was sure to win. On the map, the new boundary lines formed the shape of a salamander's body. Someone said it should be called a "gerrymander." Since the boundary changes were illegal, the new word was not meant as a compliment for Governor Gerry.

Today, we use the word "gerrymandering" to mean the redrawing of riding boundaries to ensure votes for one party. This is a way of fixing the vote and is illegal. Thanks to the Electoral Boundaries Commission Act of 1964, gerrymandering is just about extinct in Canada.

You might be accused of gerrymandering on your next birthday if you're seen cutting around those icing roses to make sure your best friend gets plenty of them. Beware!

Let's Have a Party!

WHAT DO YOU THINK OF WHEN YOU HEAR THE word "party"? Balloons, plenty of fantastic food, music and friends? You can find all of these things during an election, but you'll also find other kinds of parties — *political* parties.

In the early days of Canadian history there were no political parties. Before 1810, each candidate asked the voters to support him alone, not a party. Today, there are three major parties — the Liberal Party, the Progressive Conservative Party and the New Democratic Party — plus a number of smaller parties.

We inherited the Liberal and Conservative parties from England. The Conservatives are still sometimes called Tories: in the 1600s the Irish word *toraidhe* (pronounced tory) meant "outlaw." From 1689, Tory was the name of one of the political parties in England. The Tories supported the authority of the government and opposed religious liberty. Times changed and so did the politics. The name "Tory" was changed in 1830 to "Conservative."

The Liberals descended from the British Whigs. The Whigs opposed the Tories. For example, they supported the American Revolution against England in the 1700s while the Tories opposed it.

The New Democratic Party (NDP) is the baby of the major political parties in Canada. The NDP is a descendant of the Co-operative Commonwealth Federation (CCF), a party that was founded in Alberta in 1932.

During the Great Depression some Canadians felt they were not getting enough help from either the Conservative or the Liberal parties so the CCF was formed. Party members believed that government money should be more fairly distributed to the poorer Canadians. Farmers were especially happy about the CCF's plans for health and unemployment insurance.

But some people were afraid of the CCF because they thought it was a Communist party. Because voters were fearful, the party lost support. But in 1961, the CCF freshened its image and was reborn as the New Democratic Party.

Today members of the three parties keep after each other, constantly challenging each party and pushing for changes.

The Social Credit Party

The Great Depression also gave Canada the Social Credit Party, in 1932. Members of this party wanted to give away money (called social credit) so people could buy items and services. The buyers would be supporting businesses and keeping the economy going.

The party was led by a colourful personality named William "Bible Bill" Aberhart, an Alberta evangelist. Aberhart used his radio program (remember, this was before television!) to convince his Alberta listeners to join the Social Credit Party and get instant relief from the Depression. If you were starving you'd be interested in joining, wouldn't you?

People liked what they heard and they joined the party. In the 1935 provincial election, the Socreds, as they were called, won 56 out of 63 seats. But after the election no money was actually given out. Aberhart died in 1943 but the Socreds continued to win seats until 1971. By the early 1980s, the Social Credit Party was no longer alive in Alberta and broke up there. The party is still active in British Columbia.

Watch Out! There's a Rhino at the Polls!

In many elections in Canada there have been other parties with candidates running for office. The Reform Party, Action Canada, the Communist Party of Canada and the Reconstruction Party have all fielded candidates. There have even been Rhinoceros Party candidates.

The Rhinoceros Party was started in Montreal in 1963 by people who wanted to poke fun at election campaigns. A rhino is thick-skinned, clumsy and stupid but can move fast when it senses danger. Rhino Party members thought this description fit a lot of politicians.

Rhino candidates sometimes dressed as clowns and the party's platforms were unusual. During some elections Rhinos promised the use of nuclear-powered toothbrushes, wanted to move the Rockies to central Canada and asked for the repeal of the law of gravity. From 1963 to 1984, Rhino candidates participated in all of Canada's federal elections. In 1984, believe it or not, 99,207 Canadians voted for Rhino candidates.

The Rhinoceros Party died in 1985 after the death of its founder, Dr. Jacques Ferron. One of the party's last events was a Victoria Day garage sale to sell off Rhino knick-knacks.

The Parti Québécois

The Parti Québécois started in Quebec in 1968, mainly because many French Canadians wanted independence from the rest of Canada. The Parti Québécois pushed for sovereignty association for the province. This meant that Quebec would have a status equal to that of the Government of Canada. René Lévesque was the leader of the party. Although Parti Québécois candidates were elected to Quebec's parliament, the National Assembly, and had lots of support, the question of sovereignty association was rejected by the voters in 1980 in a referendum.

Don't Kick Sand!

Sometimes we say that somebody has "real grit." Grit (American slang) means determination, stamina. In Canadian politics, members of the Liberal Party were called Clear-Grits in the 1880s. Since grit is also a bit of dirt or sand, the name gave party members a nasty image. Like sand in your eyes, the Liberals were considered pure nuisances by the Conservatives.

Parliament

LET'S SAY YOU'VE ELECTED BOB BAYOBAB TO Parliament. What exactly is Parliament and what's Bob going to do there?

Parliament is something we've inherited from England. Long ago, English kings ruled with the help of a group of nobles called the Witan. These men made the laws and gave the king money and manpower. Later, kings found they needed more money than the Witan could provide and they called upon the rest of their subjects to help. Of course, *all* the people in England couldn't go to the king. Representatives were sent and they formed the parts of the

British Parliament: the House of Lords (the nobles) and the House of Commons (the "common" men).

Canada's Parliament is based on the English model. It consists of two parts, the House of Commons and the Senate. Members of the House of Commons are elected by voters. Senators are appointed by the prime minister. Some people argue that Senators should be *elected*, rather than *appointed*.

What's Bob Bayobab going to do in Parliament?

First he'll head for the House of Commons, the house he's been elected to serve in. Members of Parliament, called MPs for short, serve their riding constituents by attending daily sessions of Parliament. Bob will ask questions, debate issues such as acid rain and vote on laws. MPs also serve on committees that examine certain issues in detail. For example, Bob sits on the pollution committee. As well, MPs help their constituents needing assistance or advice. If he's doing his job well, Bob will be very busy looking after your interests while he's in Ottawa.

Who's on Left?

When you listen to people talking politics, you'll hear the directions "left" and "right" used. What on earth do these directions have to do with government?

During the French Revolution (1789-1799), King Louis XVI held meetings with the citizens. The nobles sat on the king's right at the table, while the priests and middle classes sat on his left. (You'll notice the lower classes were not represented at all, hence the Revolution!)

After the overthrow of King Louis, the government followed the same general pattern. Members who supported tradition sat on the right, and those who supported social equality sat on the left. Today, some people say that most Conservatives are on the right, that Liberals are in the middle and that the New Democratic Party is on the left. Although, just to confuse things, there can be left-leaning Conservatives and right-leaning Liberals.

Majority/Minority

After an election you will hear the words "majority" and "minority" a lot. The party that elects the most candidates is asked by the governor general to form a government. If the government party wins more than half the seats, it is called a *majority government*.

In a majority government it is a lot easier for the government to get what it wants. Think about it. You and nine of your pizza-loving friends have enough money to buy one large pizza. If the *majority* of your friends love anchovies but you don't, you can be sure you'll be picking anchovies off your slice! You're outnumbered.

Some people say a majority government can get spoiled and lazy because it doesn't need to win support from other parties; it automatically gets what it wants. Constant examination and questioning by the other parties help keep the government attentive to the needs of the voters.

A *minority government* is formed when the government has fewer than half the seats but more seats than any

other single party. Minority governments often have a difficult time. The other parties can join forces and vote against everything the government wants. To keep this from happening, the government has to work harder to convince the other parties.

Bob may take on more responsibilities, too. If his party forms the government, he may be asked by the prime minister to take a position in the *Cabinet*. This special group of ministers looks after the various government departments. The prime minister decides who gets which department, and the ministers act as advisors to him. (Bob is being considered for Minister of the Environment because he's had so much to say about pollution.)

Talk, Talk, Talk

The word "parliament" comes from the Latin word "parliamentum" which means "to talk." When you watch the parliamentary debates on television, you'll notice that members *do* talk a lot! They present ideas, argue back and forth and sometimes swear. Every word, even the naughty ones, is taken down by special parliamentary reporters for history — and for you. This record of what was said is called *Hansard*, after T.C. Hansard, the printer of the British parliamentary debates from 1812 until 1892.

Parliamentarians are talkative! A year's worth of talk in the Ontario legislature takes up an average 8,000 pages of *Hansard*. One year, Ontario MPs filled 20,000 pages!

How do *Hansard* reporters keep track of all those words?

In the federal Parliament, the debates are taken down by shorthand stenographers who work for ten-minute shifts. Next, their shorthand is dictated to typists. All debates are taped, but the tapes are used only if someone questions the printed copy. By nine o'clock the next morning, a completed copy of everything said is printed and ready to read.

You can read through *Hansard* and find out what Bob Bayobab has said about certain issues. Then you can decide whether or not to support his re-election.

If Bob's party comes second in the election, he'll be in the Opposition. His party leader may ask Bob to be in the *Shadow Cabinet*. For example, Bob may be selected to "shadow" the Minister of the Environment. He'll be expected to keep up to date on environmental issues and aim questions at the minister while Parliament is in session.

Watch Out for Mrs. Smith!

IN MOST GROUPS THERE'S SOMEONE WHO DECIDES to disregard the rules and do his or her own thing. Maybe Jonas takes two Cokes when he's been asked to keep it to one. Maybe Kate takes a look at your paper during the exam. They don't think they're hurting anyone — maybe they're just not thinking at all. But the rules are there for a reason. If people take two Cokes, there won't be enough for everyone; if Kate gets an unusually high test score and the marks are done on a curve, your grade may be lower than it would have been. You've been cheated!

Cheating (fraud) can take place during an election, too. No one likes to admit it does, but it does. Close monitoring by electoral officials keeps the cheating in check. But some people, like Mrs. Smith, are very determined to do whatever it takes to get their candidate elected.

Ballot stuffing — Mrs. Smith steals ballots and votes more than once in the election.

Telegraphing — Heavily disguised (she thinks she's an actress!), Mrs. Smith goes to the polling station and pretends to be Mrs. Jones, who is a registered voter.

Treating — Mrs. Smith, with more money than brains, offers a few dollars to John Doe. But there's a hitch. John Doe has to vote for Mrs. Smith's candidate. Today such bribery is not found too often simply because it is very expensive. And with a secret ballot, how will Mrs. Smith know if John voted for her choice?

False enumeration — Mrs. Smith, sweet woman, volunteers to be an enumerator. Then she decides to leave off the voters' list any voter she knows will vote against her candidate. She also adds the names of under-age voters, including a few babies. She'll vote in their place.

During elections in the 1940s women were bribed with stockings because hosiery was so scarce during World War II.

(Remember the Toronto dog who almost voted?)

Padding — Mrs. Smith pads the voters' list by listing voters who don't exist. She adds invented names and the names of people who have died.

Brute force — Mrs. Smith has been known to batter a voter with her umbrella in order to "convince" him to change his vote.

It goes without saying — anyone who participates in these types of fraud will be prosecuted. Watch out, Mrs. Smith!

Denied the Right to Vote!

Imagine you've just turned 18 and you're excited about voting. The election has been called and two enumerators come to your door. This is it! You'll get on the voters' list and be able to vote.

"Oh, I'm sorry," one of the enumerators says. "You said your name is Sylvia Chang?"

"Yes," you answer proudly, waiting for any other questions.

"Yes, dear? Well, I *am* sorry," says the other enumerator. "You're of Chinese ancestry, so you can't vote. Maybe the laws will change before the next election."

Today the idea of being discriminated against just because of your ancestry seems crazy. There are laws to make sure it can't happen. But not too long ago, voter discrimination was a fact in Canada.

The Chinese
During the 1800s, many Chinese labourers were brought to Canada to lay the tracks for Canada's transcontinental railroad. They worked long hours in dangerous conditions. Prime Minister John A. Macdonald, a chief promoter of the railroad, said the Chinese were fine in Canada as labourers, but it would be unfortunate if they became permanent residents and had the right to vote.

Imagine if all blond Canadians more than six feet tall were denied the right to vote! The government would be pressured by citizens to change its stand right away. But many Canadians shared Macdonald's beliefs, and Asians were not allowed to vote for many years. Chinese Canadians and East Indian Canadians gained the vote in federal and provincial elections in 1947. The first Chinese-Canadian MP was elected in 1957.

Native Peoples

Native peoples living on Canadian reserves were not allowed to vote in a federal election until 1960, about the time your parents were children. The right to vote in *provincial* elections came even later for some Native peoples. Those on reserves in Alberta got the provincial vote in 1965; in Quebec, the Native peoples have voted in provincial elections for only the last 20 years. That's about 200 years after the first votes were cast in Canada!

The Inuit were ignored by the government until 1939 — and they still did not get the vote until 1950. Now Inuit are active in local, territorial and federal politics.

The Japanese

The Japanese came to Canada in the late 1800s and settled mainly on the west coast. They were denied the right to vote even though they were very active members of Canadian society.

The sons and daughters of these immigrants were born in Canada but they were still denied the vote simply because of their culture. During World War II, when Canada joined the war against Germany and Japan, the Japanese Canadians were placed in internment camps. Their property was taken by the Canadian government and was not returned, even after the war was over. (A good story about a family in the camps is *Naomi's Road* by Joy Kogawa.)

These people were punished only because they shared a heritage with the enemy. It wasn't until 1949, after the war, that Japanese Canadians were granted the right to vote.

The Mennonites

A similar kind of discrimination happened to the Mennonites during World War I. The Mennonites were members of a religious sect, centred in Germany, who came to America in the 1700s. Many settled in Manitoba and Southern Ontario.

After Britain declared war on Germany in 1914, the Mennonites were accused of being spies for Germany, just because they spoke German. The government took away their right to vote in the 1917 election and didn't restore it until the 1920s. Imagine having the vote for one election and then having it taken away in the next!

Today, some Old Order Mennonites are opposed to holding public office, but others, like the Conference Mennonites, run for and win public offices.

Thank You, Nurses!

IF IT WEREN'T FOR THE NURSES WHO RISKED THEIR lives in World War I, Canadian women might still be waiting for the right to vote. Before the war the saying, "No woman, idiot, lunatic or criminal shall vote" outraged women. One politician asked, "What in the world do women want to vote for?... My mother was the best woman in the world and she certainly never wanted to vote!"

Around 1910, Canadian women started to demand the vote. Women who spoke out and battled for the right to vote were called *suffragettes*. (Suffrage, like *franchise*, is the right or privilege of voting.) Meetings of suffragettes and their supporters were held all over the world. The result? Riots, arrests, prison and for some, death.

Then came the war. Conscription, or the compulsory drafting of men into the armed forces, was the major issue in the 1917 election. Prime Minister Robert Borden wanted to make sure that his government and its

conscription plans got the voters' support. He thought the patriotic women nurses overseas would back him, so he gave them the vote. To be safe, Borden took the vote away from foreign-born Canadians, unless they had a son, grandson, or brother serving in battle and instead gave the vote to the wives, mothers and sisters of servicemen. Women were allowed to vote in a federal election for the first time. You can guess what happened. Borden and his government won the election.

During the war, people who were against the idea of women voting began to change their minds. Thousands of men left their jobs and went to Europe to fight. That left women with extra responsibilities. They had to keep their homes and families going *and* they had to work outside the home to help the war effort and keep Canada going. People began to feel that women deserved a say in how the government worked.

Now You Have It, Now You Don't

SOME WOMEN IN THE MARITIMES AND QUEBEC HAD the vote in the late 1700s and early 1800s, but lost the vote later: after Confederation in 1867 men could vote and women no longer could. (When the right to vote is taken away it is called *disenfranchisement*.) The same Sir John A. Macdonald who denied the Chinese citizenship tried to get the vote for women in the 1880s. But he failed. By 1900, Canadian women could vote in municipal elections and become school trustees in some cities. But they were still denied a vote for the government of Canada.

Three strong women battled over the years for the Canadian woman's right to vote in every election and to hold office. Of course, they weren't the only supporters of women's rights, but they were among the most outspoken. They appeared at government meetings, wrote for newspapers and made public appearances. Radio and, later, television gave McClung, Mcphail and Casgrain maximum exposure to the people, and helped these women bring about something quite extraordinary — the chance for every woman to help shape Canada's government.

Nellie McClung (1873 - 1951)

Nellie Mooney McClung was born in Ontario but grew up in Manitoba. She began to teach school when she was 16 and later wrote books. McClung married a druggist and together they raised five children. Still she had time to work in a temperance society (a group that tried to stop the sale of alcoholic beverages). After her family moved to Winnipeg in 1911, McClung found she was invited to speak more often about women's suffrage and after yet another family move, to Edmonton, she continued her

NELLIE McCLUNG

fight for women's rights.

McClung served as a member of the legislative assembly for five years before moving to Vancouver and continuing her suffrage efforts. She was a humorous, convincing public speaker who was never afraid to challenge politicians.

Agnes Mcphail (1890 - 1954)

Agnes Campbell Mcphail was the first woman elected to the federal House of Commons after Canadian women gained the right to vote. She served in the House from 1921 until 1940 and in 1943 became one of the first women elected to the Ontario legislature.

Like McClung, Mcphail was born in Ontario and taught school when she was very young. Her political career included being a founder of the CCF Party in 1932. Agnes Mcphail worked hard for prison reform, farm issues and equal pay legislation. She died just before her appointment to the Senate was announced.

AGNES MCPHAIL   THÉRÈSE CASGRAIN

Thérèse Casgrain (1896 - 1981)

Women voters in Quebec owe a great deal of thanks to Thérèse Forget Casgrain. She was born to a wealthy family in Montreal, married a lawyer and raised four children. She was a founding member of the Provincial Franchise Committee in 1921 and helped Québécois women get the right to vote provincially in 1940. Thérèse Casgrain was provincial leader of the CCF Party in the 1950s and was appointed to the Senate in 1970.

Steps in the Right Direction

1916 Manitoba becomes the first province to allow women to vote in provincial elections. Saskatchewan and Alberta follow.

1917 The Military Voters Act gives war nurses the federal vote. The Wartime Elections Act grants the vote to wives, mothers and sisters of servicemen. Ontario and British Columbia grant women provincial voting rights.

1918 Women aged 21 and older are granted the right to vote in federal elections.

1919 Women can stand for seats in the House of Commons.

1940 Quebec becomes the last province to give women the vote.

Lessons from History

FASCINATING PICTURES OF LIFE LONG AGO CAN BE found in old newspapers, poll books and political pamphlets from past elections. Old poll books, usually kept in a town or city hall, are lists of voters and their addresses and occupations. Take the City of Toronto Poll Book for 1841, for example.

Each voter is identified by his occupation. (You'll only see the names of the men; women weren't allowed to vote yet.) There were blacksmiths and whitesmiths. (A whitesmith is a worker in "white iron," or tin.) Toronto in 1841 had 90 builders and carpenters, one undertaker (listed under carpenters) and eight ministers. Three people made soap and candles for the city and kept light in the taverns run by 67 tavern keepers. Only seven male teachers served all the children who were allowed to go to school and nine coach-makers, wagon-makers and wheel-wrights kept Toronto moving. If you were wealthy enough to buy a piano there was only one man who could build it. Some of the voters' names will bring a smile to your face. Charles Clinkinbroomer was a watch-maker with a great name!

After each name there are the initials of the candidates for whom the man voted. You could look at the poll book and see who your neighbourhood butcher voted for. If it wasn't *your* candidate, you might take your business to another butcher.

According to the poll book, voting lasted for seven days, instead of one day as it does today, and the tally for each day's vote was recorded. If your candidate was losing on Tuesday, you could try to drum up support for the other voting days.

A Ballot with a Beer Chaser

Long ago, the local tavern was a general meeting place for the neighbourhood, so it was only natural that voting should take place there. Tables were set up outside the tavern for the election.

Finding supporters could be an expensive, sometimes nasty business. Servants were sometimes forced by their employers to vote for certain candidates. Bribery of tavern keepers was common and there was always lots of whiskey around to keep voters happy. A vote could be bought for the price of a whiskey punch. When the final votes were tallied, the victorious candidate was sometimes hoisted on a tavern chair above the heads of his supporters and carried around the town. Imagine the noise of the celebrating winners and the drinking done by the losers who wanted to forget the election. Often, there were riots between the two groups and sometimes innocent bystanders were killed during the scuffles.

An election in Montreal in 1832 left a man named François Languedoc dead on the street. Newspapermen saw Languedoc's death as a reason to stay home during an election. They reported:

"Languedoc yielded to the repeated importunities of his friends and went to the poll. He had never made a practice of attending elections and was a remarkably peaceful man; but in an unfortunate moment went to the poll on

Monday, arrived at the time of the riot and in a few minutes he was numbered with the dead."

Laws that curbed the riots were eventually passed. During the hours a polling station was open for a provincial election, no one could buy liquor. This law was abolished in 1975 because it was outdated — politicians were not buying votes with liquor anymore. On federal election day, however, no one can buy liquor during voting hours. The government is considering updating this law, too.

See How They Run

ONCE A FEDERAL ELECTION HAS BEEN CALLED AND an election day is set, the countdown begins.

There is a minimum of 50 days before people vote and there's plenty to be done. Election day is called "Day 0" and "Day 28" is Nomination Day. On that day, a list with the names of every candidate in Canada is drawn up.

How do candidates get nominated?

Any person who is a qualified voter can run for office. The candidate may seek election in only one electoral district at a time.

A candidate who wants to represent a political party must win the support of that party: this is usually done at a nomination meeting held by party members in the electoral district. A candidate who is not endorsed by a party can run as an independent candidate. But that's only the beginning.

Let's say Tiffany Lampe wants to be an MP for the Edisonville district. She must have an official agent (who handles all the financial transactions of the campaign) and an auditor (someone who will check financial reports). The returning officer in the district will give Tiffany official nomination papers. To be nominated officially, she needs at least 25 signatures of voters who live in the Edisonville district. All Tiffany's nomination papers must be completed and turned in by 2 P.M. on Day 28. She also needs to make a money deposit to show she's serious about running for office.

At the end of Day 28, if Tiffany is the only candidate, the returning officer will close the election and declare her the winner by *acclamation*.

It was easy for Tiffany, wasn't it? For most candidates there's a great deal more work.

Come to the Toga Party!

The word *candidate* comes from the Latin word meaning "clothed in white." Why? Long ago in ancient Rome, men who wished to be elected or appointed to office wore white togas. Imagine if modern-day candidates dressed in white togas on election day!

Let's say two other people decide to run against Tiffany Lampe. She'll have to campaign to win voters' support. She'll choose a *campaign manager* to oversee every detail of her campaign. Tiffany will need someone who has a lot of campaign experience. The manager will see that a headquarters is set up, maybe in a vacant store. He or she will make sure Tiff gets to the opening of that new seniors' centre and that she has her picture taken kissing a cute baby. It's important for Tiffany to be known by voters. The manager will also arrange fund-raising dinners so the money will keep coming in and will hire speech-writers to help Tiffany present her ideas well to the voters.

Campaigning is hard work. Tiffany will have to go

Wanderlust

Prime Minister Sir Wilfrid Laurier was the first party leader ever to visit the western provinces during a federal campaign. That was in 1917, and he travelled by train. Candidates now need a faster way of getting around so they fly thousands of kilometres to see voters in hard-to-reach parts of Canada. Sir John A. Macdonald might have seen a thousand voters during a campaign; today's politicians see hundreds of thousands in just 50 days.

mainstreeting: she'll stroll through shopping malls or down busy streets in her area, shaking hands and chatting with voters. She wants to get to know the voters and let them get to know her. What are their concerns? How can she help them?

By the time Tiffany Lampe is elected, she may have gained 5 kilograms (11 pounds) from too much fast food and too many benefit dinner banquets. She may have dark circles under her eyes from lack of sleep after late-night speeches. And her family may hardly recognize her because she's hardly been home. But it's all part of a candidate's life and Tiffany Lampe hopes that on election day her efforts will result in victory.

Slogans

When you urge your school team on to victory at the hockey play-offs, you cheer, "Go get 'em, Rivercrest!" or whatever your school is called. This slogan whips up team spirit. Election slogans work the same way. Long ago slogans were the battle cries of warriors; now slogans appear on election posters, television commercials and buttons.

Here are some slogans from past elections:

"By a Party, with a Party, but for a Country" (Sir John A. Macdonald, 1875)

"Let Laurier Finish His Work" (Sir Wilfrid Laurier, 1908)
"King or Chaos" (William Lyon Mackenzie King, 1935)
"Peace, Progress and Pearson" (Lester Pearson, 1957)
"Trudeau and One Canada" (Pierre Elliot Trudeau, 1968)

Notice that the name of the candidate is usually part of the slogan. Some candidates today hire advertising agencies to create election slogans that will keep their names in the voters' minds right until election day.

"Getting to Know You..."

 WHEN TIFFANY LAMPE ANNOUNCED HER CANDIDACY in your riding, maybe you'd never heard of her before. Why should you give her your vote? She's just a name to you. How can you get more information about her?

Choosing a candidate can be difficult. Candidates from different political parties often say basically the same thing. After all, no candidate is going to say he or she doesn't care about acid rain. Listen carefully. Tiffany may propose a quick solution. Mr. C. may say acid rain is not a top priority issue; the budget is his concern.

How do you find out what Tiffany and the other candidates stand for? Campaign literature is one guide. Political parties and candidates print tonnes of brochures. Usually these feature biographies of the candidates and outline key election topics.

Local and national newspapers are filled with articles and editorials about candidates and what they think. And television can let you see some parliamentarians in action. If Mr. C. is running for re-election, you may want to see how he performs daily in Ottawa, on television. You might also read what he's said in *Hansard* (see page 27).

You can also talk to Tiffany face to face. Candidates visit neighbourhoods to talk to the voters. Tiffany may knock on your door or attend a community picnic. That's your chance to ask her what she really feels about issues of concern to you.

Building a New Government

A *plank* of the candidate's platform is a single item of the party's plan of action. Solutions for the homeless, for example, might be one major plank of a candidate's platform.

These building words remind us of the early days of campaigning when politicians stood on wooden platforms high above the crowds and delivered fiery speeches.

If you want to see how Tiffany's ideas compare to those of other candidates, go to an all-candidates meeting. Voters can listen to speeches by all of the candidates in the area and ask questions. Ready to decide? Which candidate will receive your vote on Day 0?

Run for the Money

IT TAKES A LOT OF MONEY TO RUN A CAMPAIGN. There are offices to maintain, cars and chairs to rent, paper-clips, pens, stickers to buy, signs and brochures to print and people to hire. Even grocery items like coffee and sugar have to be figured into the cost of a campaign. Volunteer supporters do much of the work but still there are bills, bills, bills.

What would happen if a very wealthy candidate ran against a poor one? Wouldn't the wealthy one have a better chance of winning because he or she could buy more television ads or larger signs?

Not necessarily.

By law, candidates and their parties can spend only a certain amount on an election campaign. These spending limits are determined by the number of voters in each candidate's riding. In large ridings, candidates are granted extra funds because of the high cost of travel.

The political parties also have limits to what they can spend. These limits are based on the number of voters in

the ridings in which they are running candidates. In 1988, the largest parties were limited to about $8 million each.

After the election, parties and candidates must reveal the source of campaign contributions. They must identify any person or group who gives more than $100 to a party in any given year or to a candidate in an election. Otherwise, someone might try to slip a few extra million dollars to a candidate in return for future favours.

Perhaps your family wants to contribute big bucks to a particular party or candidate. If you want to fill a suitcase with shiny loonies and lug it down to your candidate's office, you can. But you'll have to get an official receipt for all that cash. What will you get in return for your money? Forget about special favours. Instead, you'll get a tax credit from the government. This "reward" encourages voters to give more than votes to the candidates they admire.

Animal Farm

Listen to the radio during an election and you might think you've stumbled into a barnyard. You'll hear about ducks, dogs, lambs and horses. Here's a guide to who's who.

Dark Horse
Sometimes people believe a candidate has no chance at all of winning. Then on election day, surprise! In horse racing, the same thing happens. Most of the bets have been placed on, say, Greased Lightning, but Old Fred wins the race. The candidate who comes "from nowhere" and wins the election is the dark horse.

The horse-racing expression "running neck-and-neck" is also used during a campaign or on election day. It means the candidates are within a few votes of each other.

RE-ELECT GREASED LIGHTNING

VOTE FOR OLD FRED

Sacrificial Lamb

If a very popular candidate is running for re-election, the chances of beating her may be slim. A candidate who runs against her is almost sure to lose. He or she is a "sacrificial lamb."

Why be a sacrificial lamb? To gain experience and perhaps be rewarded by the party with an appointment or support in another election.

Underdog

During a campaign, voters are sometimes asked their opinion about who will win. The results of these *public opinion polls* let people know who is in the lead before election day. The "underdog" is the losing party or candidate. Just because a candidate is called the underdog a few weeks before election day doesn't mean he or she will lose the election. Voters can change their minds right up until they mark their ballots!

Lame Duck

A prime minister who announces he's retiring can expect to be called a lame duck. He is still in power, but everyone knows he's on the way out. Voters don't pay as much attention to a politician in this position, so it's more difficult for him to get things done. Like a duck who can't fly, he is unable to make any progress. Voters are looking ahead to the next prime minister, who they hope will give them what they want and need.

Pork-barrelling

This is when members of government give out jobs or contracts to supporters rather than to others who might be better qualified or more deserving. Sometimes, this is how sacrificial lambs are rewarded. Pork-barrelling is also called political patronage.

"How Do I Look?"

WHEN YOU GO TO APPLY FOR A JOB AT THE hardware store, you don't spray your hair green and wear a ripped T-shirt — and expect to get the job. You dress for success. First impressions are important in elections too, and candidates spend lots of time and money "improving their images" before meeting voters.

Television brings candidates into voters' living rooms. Candidates who "look bad" on TV hire media experts to groom them for appearances. Some candidates get complete make-overs, everything from a new hairdo and contact lenses to a snappier wardrobe.

During federal elections, political parties produce television commercials, and they want their candidates to "project" well. (These commercials are broadcast during the last four weeks before election day. Advertising is banned for the 24 hours before the polls open.)

Some candidates have trademarks — certain items that become identified with them. Prime Minister Lester Pearson wore bow-ties, Prime Minister Pierre Trudeau often sported a rose in his lapel and Ontario Premier David Peterson wore red neckties. These trademarks help politicians set themselves apart from the rest of the pack and give you something to remember.

JOHN A. MACDONALD

WILFRID LAURIER

BRIAN MULRONEY

Funny Faces

Sometimes it's part of a candidate's face that becomes his or her trademark. For example, Prime Minister Brian Mulroney is known for his chin. During elections, political cartoonists fill editorial pages with their funny, but meaningful, comments on the candidates and events. These caricatures exaggerate a candidate's facial features and can replace the real image of the person in people's minds.

Political cartooning has been going on for hundreds, maybe even thousands, of years. Canada's first prime minister, Sir John A. Macdonald, was caricatured weekly by cartoonist J.W. Bengough. For many people today, Bengough's cartoon is still their picture of Macdonald. Bengough started his own magazine, filled with this kind of cartoon, and kept his readers laughing *and* informed about every bit of the prime minister's career. Check out the editorial page of *your* local paper — and be prepared to chuckle!

Say It Louder, Please!

The secret ballot is also called an Australian Ballot because the Australians pioneered its use in 1858.

A HUNDRED AND FIFTY YEARS AGO WHEN YOU voted (remember, only men could vote) you called the name of your choice *out loud* in front of the candidates and all of their supporters. An election clerk wrote down your choice. This method was called *viva voce*, Latin for "voting out loud." Because all voting was public, there were many opportunities for bullying and vote buying.

Merchants might say to customers who owed them money, "Vote for my man and we'll forget this debt." Or a candidate's supporters might try to buy voters by buying them drinks. In 1831, a man could buy a gallon of whiskey for only 20 cents and that could buy quite a few votes.

Back in 1831 a group of reformers wanted laws passed to clean up elections. They pushed for secret ballots — paper ballots on which the voter could write the name of his choice. (These reformers also wanted the poll locations to be closer to the people. In early days, voters had to travel for miles in poor weather on rough roads and at great expense. Because of this, many people never voted.)

Not everyone agreed with voting in secret. Some people believed it was sneaky. If you were committed to a candidate, they argued, why not proudly call out his name? Open voting was called "the manly British practice." But the reformers won. The secret ballot became law in 1874. The first secret ballot slid into a ballot box in the federal election of 1878.

Paper Power

Ballot is from an Italian word "ballotta," meaning a round bullet. In the 1500s in Venice, Italy, voters dropped a bullet-like ball into a box or urn marked with their candidate's name.

Today, millions of ballots are printed on official ballot paper. The paper contains a barely visible design called a watermark. This mark can be seen only when the paper is held to the light. It cannot be copied. If someone prints ballots on a paper without this watermark, election officials suspect tampering and destroy all the ballots. All ballots are numbered so that they can be identified and are kept under tight security before and after election day.

Voting Underwater and Under the Weather

VOTERS CAN FIND THEMSELVES IN SOME STRANGE situations on election day. What if you're in the hospital? Or in a submarine? Or out of the country? Can you still vote? Read on and find out.

You've had a sore throat for a few days and the doctor says your tonsils have to come out. The operation is scheduled for, you guessed it, election day! Don't worry

— you can still vote. The card you received in the mail after the enumerators came lists the advance polling station in your neighbourhood. Advance polls are open on the ninth, seventh and sixth days before election day.

If you're in the hospital for a longer stay or are a university student far from home and miss the advance polling days, you can vote by *proxy*. This means you can ask a friend or neighbour to vote for you. Proxy voting is allowed only on election day and your name and the name of your friend must be on the same voters' list.

Canadians who are out of the country can't vote. Or at least most of them can't. Special arrangements are made for Canadian diplomats and Armed Forces members and their families. They can vote 15 days before election day. Their secret ballots are sent back to Canada and included in the tally of votes from their riding on election day.

So whether you're in an Armed Forces submarine on the ocean bottom or an astronaut in outer space on election day, you haven't lost out. Your feet will be firmly on land when you mark your ballot before your trip!

Other Special Cases

- Blind and visually impaired people can vote, even though they can't see the ballot. A piece of stiff paper (a template) is slipped over a ballot. The circles on the ballot match up with circles cut into the template. The voter feels these circles to find out where to make his or her mark. The poll official may be asked to tell the voter the order of the names on the ballot.
- Illiterate voters (those who can't read) or voters who are physically handicapped (perhaps they cannot use their hands) can bring a friend to help them vote. Special oaths are taken and the voter and friend can then go to the booth together to mark the ballot or the deputy returning officer can help the voter.
- Voters who don't speak English or French sometimes ask for help from an interpreter. Interpreters must take an oath before translating the election officer's instructions about marking a ballot. The interpreter does not go behind the screen with the voter.

Election Day at Last!

Whoops!

If you accidentally rip your ballot or mark it incorrectly, you'll be given a new one. The officer will write "spoiled" on the ripped ballot and will keep it apart from the other ballots in the ballot box. Ballots are rejected during counting if a voter puts two marks instead of one, or writes over the candidate's name, instead of in the circle, or writes on the ballot with any mark other than an X.

WEEKS OF WORK HAVE GONE INTO THE ELECTION and the polling stations are ready to open. From 9 A.M. to 8 P.M. voters will be able to mark their ballots. No campaign literature or party supporters are allowed near or in the station; no one can put pressure on a voter as he or she enters to vote.

Let's imagine you're a first-time voter and walk through the voting procedure. You may be surprised at how simple it is!

As you enter the polling station, the first thing you'll see are two people sitting behind a table — the *deputy returning officer* (DRO) and a *poll clerk*. The poll clerk finds your name on the voters' list, marks it off and enters your name in the poll book record. The DRO is in charge at the polling station and gives you a folded ballot, which he or she has already initialled on the back. You'll then go behind a cardboard voting screen placed on a table.

Now what?

Listed on the ballot are the candidates' names and parties. The names are listed alphabetically. Beside each name is a blank circle. You will mark with an X one circle of the ballot and return it, folded, to the officer.

Forgot your pen? Don't worry. Pencils are provided at each voting screen.

When you hand your marked ballot back to the DRO, she checks to make sure it is the same ballot she gave you. She does this by looking at the initials she put on the ballot earlier. Then she puts your ballot in the ballot box. She does not see which candidate you marked.

The poll clerk writes "voted" next to your name in the poll book.

Congratulations! You have just finished voting for the first time!

Aaron Aardvark

Some people say that there is an advantage to being named Aaron Aardvark if you are running for office. Your name will be the first on the ballot. When there isn't a favourite candidate in an election, the first name on the ballot tends to get more votes!

ELECT AARON AARDVARK

Alderman- WARD 6

Who Can Work at the Polls?

You may be interested in politics. Perhaps you're thinking about a career as a politician. You're 16 and you already have a job at Bobo's Burgers so you're certainly old enough to work at a polling station and learn how it all works.

Not so.

The people who are hired to work at polling stations have to be eligible voters, so they all have to be at least 18. Many people think this is unfair. They argue that if young people become more involved in government *before* they turn 18, they might be more interested in what is going on when they *can* vote.

Some election workers under age 18 can be appointed, under very special circumstances. For example, if there's a shortage of enumerators, people under age 18 can take on the job. So there's hope that the age rules for polling station workers may change, too.

What? No Time to Vote?

Every voter in Canada is entitled to have four consecutive hours to vote on election day. This may involve taking some time off work. A boss cannot punish any worker who leaves to vote. But he may decide what four hours employees can be gone. All the nurses at a hospital can't leave at the same time to vote!

Scrutinizing the Situation

When you enter the polling station, you may see some people sitting near the DRO and the poll clerk. These are the *scrutineers*. They observe carefully, or "scrutinize," the voting proceedings to make sure everything is following the law.

Scrutineers are appointed by the candidates to work at the station on their behalf. They may examine the poll book as election day progresses to see who has voted. If John Green, one of the candidate's strongest supporters, hasn't voted yet, the scrutineer may relay information to the campaign office. People there can call Mr. Green and see if he needs a ride to the polls, a babysitter, whatever. They need his vote. A scrutineer can leave and re-enter the station as he pleases and can challenge a voter's right to vote. But he cannot question any voter or influence a voter's decision.

After the Doors Close

YOU'VE VOTED, SO YOUR WORK ON ELECTION DAY IS done. But there are others who keep working after the polling station doors are locked. That's when the vote counting starts.

The ballot box, which has been sealed shut during the day, is opened and all the ballots are emptied onto a table. Only the deputy returning officer (DRO) can handle the ballots and he or she is closely watched by the

DRO   SCRUTINEERS   POLL CLERK

LING   SMITH   LAMPE   KLEIN

scrutineers. The DRO picks up each ballot, checks the initials on the back and calls out the name of the candidate marked on it. The ballot is shown to the scrutineers and the poll clerk. A separate pile is kept for each candidate. Unmarked, rejected and spoiled ballots are also put into separate piles and counted.

The poll clerk and scrutineers keep score on the official tally sheets provided by Elections Canada. Ballots are rejected if a voter put two marks instead of one, or wrote over the candidate's name, not in the circles. The total number of ballots counted must equal the number of names registered by the clerk in the poll book.

To prevent voters from being influenced by early votes, the ballots from the advance polling days are not counted until the polls close on election day. The DRO counts these votes, too. In some municipal elections, computers tally the votes, but officials are finding problems with this method. Costly and frustrating recounts become necessary when the machines malfunction.

When the ballot count and the poll book count match, the DRO completes and certifies an official statement of the votes. The ballots are never counted again unless a recount is granted later. Each scrutineer is given a certificate of the count. A closing oath is taken by the poll officials and the documents are placed in the ballot box with all the ballots. The box is sealed with a new set of seals and taken or sent back to the returning officer. Meanwhile, the DROs at various polls phone in their results to the returning officer. The media and the people

Oh No! Not Again!

A recount is automatically conducted by a judge if the winning candidate won by fewer than 25 votes. A recount may also be held if the results are very close and one candidate requests a recount. If there is a tie, the returning officer can vote and break the tie. Otherwise the returning officer cannot vote.

It's Official!

After all the ballot boxes have been returned, the returning officer double checks the count on the official statements in each box. If there isn't a request for recount within seven days, the returning officer completes the election writ and notifies the chief electoral officer of the name of the winning candidate. A copy of the notice is given to each candidate. Candidates cannot be sworn in until the returning officer has sent the writ of election back to the chief electoral officer.

at party headquarters will soon know the final tabulations, but these will only be *unofficial* results.

After the winners are declared, reports have to be filed with Elections Canada. All the ballots, used and unused, are sent to Ottawa where Elections Canada keeps them for one year and then destroys every ballot. Candidates, winners and losers, have to submit to the returning officer an account of all the money they spent and received for the transmission to Elections Canada. Constituency offices for the newly elected members of Parliament have to be staffed on a permanent basis. Newsletters and reports have to be printed and sent to voters.

And *your* job as a voter is not done yet either. Voters should listen to and watch the people they elected. After all, the winning candidates may decide to run for re-election in future. You'll need to know if they've done well. Being a watchdog is a full-time job.

Did you ever think you could do so much just by marking an X in a circle?

Glossary

acclamation   This occurs when only one candidate files a nomination paper and is therefore declared the winner.

advance polls   These polling stations open before election day so that voters in special circumstances can vote.

Australian ballot   A secret ballot.

ballot   The special piece of paper marked by a voter.

ballot stuffing   Voting more than once in an election.

by-election   A special election held between elections in order to fill vacant provincial or federal seats.

Cabinet   A group of ministers who look after various government departments.

campaign manager   The person who oversees a candidate's election plan and manages the details.

caricature   A portrait in which the subject's features are deliberately exaggerated or distorted.

chief electoral officer (CEO)   The government official who is in charge of co-ordinating all aspects of an election.

conscription   The compulsory drafting of men into the armed forces.

constituents   Voters in a riding who are represented by an elected official.

democracy   Government by the people, either directly or through elected representatives.

deputy returning officer (DRO)   An official at the polling station on election day.

disenfranchisement   This occurs when the right to vote is taken away.

Elections Canada   A government agency responsible for the organization of all federal elections.

electoral map   A special map showing the electoral districts in a province or across the country.

enumerators   Representatives of political parties who go door to door and compile the voters' lists.

false enumeration   Tampering with the voters' lists to "fix" the election outcome.

franchise   The right or privilege to vote; also called suffrage.

Hansard   The official printed record of all that is said during parliamentary debates.

House Assembly   The provincial parliament of Newfoundland.

House of Commons   One of the sections of Parliament. The members are elected by eligible voters; also called the Lower House.

Legislative Assembly   The provincial parliament in some provinces.

majority government   A majority government occurs when the winning party has more than half the seats in Parliament.

minority government   A minority government is formed when the winning party has fewer than half the seats in Parliament but more seats than any other single party.

National Assembly   The provincial parliament in Quebec.

nomination day   Day 28 in an election countdown; the day a list with the names of the candidates is drawn up.

non-partisan   Not influenced by and not supporting any one particular party.

notice of enumeration   A card that tells the voter where and when to vote.

padding   Adding the names of non-existent voters to the voters' list.

Parliament   The federal body that makes Canadian laws. It consists of the Queen's representative (the governor general), an appointed Senate and an elected House of Commons.

platform   A candidate or party's list of plans and promises.

poll clerk   An official at the polling station.

polling station   The place where voters cast their ballots; also called the polls.

proxy vote   A vote cast by one voter on behalf of another voter.

recount   The retabulation of votes called for by a judge.

referendum   A special kind of vote that takes place when a very important public question must be decided.

responsible government   A system of government in which the prime minister and his Cabinet are responsible to Parliament, who in turn are responsible to the people.

returning officer   The key official in each electoral district.

61

riding Another word for electoral district.

scrutineer An appointed party supporter who observes the proceedings at the polling station on election day.

Senate The Upper House of Parliament made up of those appointed by the prime minister.

Shadow Cabinet A group of official opposition party spokespeople who "shadow" specific Cabinet ministers.

slogan An election cheer that sums up what the candidate or party is saying and helps whip up interest and excitement.

spoiled ballot A ballot that has been torn or marked incorrectly.

suffragette A woman who speaks out and battles for the right to vote.

voters' list A list of the people eligible to vote in an election.

Index

Aberhart, William 21
acclamation 38
Action Canada Party 22
advance polls 12, 53
Alberta 35
all-candidates meeting 43
automation 13

ballot 18, 51, 53, 54, 55, 58, 59, 60
    Australian 50
    boxes 13, 58, 59
    rejected 54
    secret 50-51
    spoiled 54
    stuffing 28
Bengough, J.W. 49
Borden, Robert 32-33
bribery 28, 37
British Columbia 21, 35
brute force 29, 37, 50
by-election 11

Cabinet 6, 12, 26
campaign manager 39
campaigning 38-45, 48, 49
candidate 15, 19-21, 36, 38, 41, 46-49,
    55, 57, 59 (see also campaigning)
caricature 49
cartooning 49
Casgrain, Thérèse 35
Charter of Rights and Freedoms 8
cheating 28-29
chief electoral officer 12-15, 59
Chinese 30
Clear-Grits 23
Commonwealth of Independent
    States 7
Communist Party (CIS) 7
Communist Party of Canada 22
computers 13, 59
conscription 11, 32
constituencies 18
Co-operative Commonwealth
    Federation (CCF) 20-21, 35

dark horse 46
democracy 6, 7
Depression 20, 21
deputy returning officer 53-55, 57-59
discrimination 30-34
disenfranchisement 31, 33, 34
donations 45

East Indians 30
Edmonton 34

election
    federal 7, 9, 12, 13, 15, 22, 30,
        33, 35, 37, 38, 48
    municipal 9, 10, 34
    provincial 9, 10, 21, 30, 31, 37
election day 15, 17, 36, 37, 38, 54-60
Elections Canada 13, 56, 59, 60
electoral boundaries 19
Electoral Boundaries Commission
    Act 19
electoral districts 12, 18, 19
electoral map 18
eligibility 7, 8-9, 38, 56
England 20, 24
enumeration 14, 16, 30, 56
    false 28

Ferron, Jacques Dr. 22
finances 44-45, 60
franchise 32
fraud 28-29
French Revolution 25

Germany 31
Gerry, Elbridge 19
gerrymandering 19
governor general 14, 15, 26

Haiti 6
Hansard 27, 42
Hansard, T.C. 27
House Assembly 10
House of Commons 25, 35
House of Lords 25

India 13
internment camps 31
interpreter 53
Inuit 31

Japanese 31
judges 8-9, 59

King, William Lyon Mackenzie 41

lame duck 47
Languedoc, François 37
Laurier, Sir Wilfrid 39, 41
'Left' 25
Legislative Assembly 10
Lévesque, René 23
Liberal Party 20, 23, 25
liquor 34, 37, 50
Louis XVI, King 25

Macdonald, Sir John A. 30, 34,
    39, 41
mainstreeting 40
majority government 26
Manitoba 31, 34, 35
McClung, Nellie 34-35
Mcphail, Agnes 35
Mennonites 31
Military Voters Act 35
minority government 26
Montreal 22, 35, 37
Mulroney, Brian 49
multiple-party system 7

Naomi's Road 31
National Assembly 10, 23
Native peoples 31
New Democratic Party 20, 25
Newfoundland 10
newspapers 17, 36, 37, 42, 49
Nomination Day 38
    papers 38
non-confidence, vote of 15
non-partisan 13
Northwest Territories 18, 19
Notice of Enumeration 17
Nova Scotia 9
Nunatsiaq 18, 19

oaths 17, 53, 59
one-party system 7
Ontario 18, 27, 31, 34, 35
Opposition 27

padding 29
Parliament 6-7, 10, 11, 13-15, 19,
    24-25, 27
Parti Québécois 23
Pearson, Lester 41, 48
Peterson, David 48
plank 43
platform 43
plebiscite 11
political cartooning 49
political parties 7, 16, 20-23, 26
    38, 44
political patronage 47
poll 18
    books 36, 54, 57, 59
    clerk 54, 55, 59
    public opinion 47
polling station 17, 19, 37, 50, 54
pork-barrelling 47
prime minister 6, 14, 15, 26, 47

Prince Edward Island 9, 18
prisoners 8
Progressive Conservative Party 20,
   23, 25
Provincial Franchise Committee 35

Quebec 9, 10, 19, 23, 31, 34, 35

radio 17, 21, 34
Reconstruction Party 22
recounts 59
re-election 27, 47, 60
referendum 11, 23
Reform Party 22
responsible government 6
returning officer 12, 13, 38, 59, 60
Rhinoceros Party 22
riding 18, 44
'Right' 25

sacrificial lamb 47
Saskatchewan 18, 35
Sauvé, Jeanne 14
scrutineers 57-59

Senate 25, 35
Shadow Cabinet 27
slogans 41
social credit 21
Social Credit Party 21
Socreds 21
sovereignty association 23
suffrage 32
suffragettes 32

taverns 37
telegraphing 28
television 17, 27, 34, 41, 42, 48, 59
temperance society 34
tie vote 59
Toronto 36
Tory 20
trademarks 48-49
travel 39
treating 28
Trudeau, Pierre Elliot 41, 48

underdog 47
United States 9

Vancouver 35
Venice 51
viva voce 50
voter fraud 28-29, 37
voter turnout 9
voters' list 8, 9, 12, 14, 16-17, 30, 54
voting 52-60
   advance 12, 53
   Armed Forces 53
   blind 53
   illiterate 53
   physically handicapped 53
   proxy 53
   registration 16
   visually impaired 53

Wartime Elections Act 35
Whig 20
Winnipeg 34
Witan 24
women 32-36
World War I 31, 32
World War II 31
writs of election 12

Yukon 18